MW01172951

Young People of the Bible

Debbie Kea

Gospel Armory
PUBLISHING

Young People of the Bible
Copyright © 2024 by Debbie Kea

All Rights Reserved. No portion of this book may be reproduced in any form without the written permission of the publisher, except in the case of brief excerpts to be used in a review.

Published by:
Gospel Armory Publishing
Bowling Green, Kentucky
www.GospelArmory.com

Printed in the United States of America

ISBN: 978-1-959201-49-6

TABLE OF CONTENTS

Note to Bible class teachers:

Each lesson is meant to be read aloud in a class period so that students can follow along and visitors can also benefit from the lessons. The discussion questions are designed to involve the whole class and invite participation from everyone present.

LESSON 1

Daniel

Imagine yourself as royalty, with all the amenities that entails, a prince with power, goods, all that position and prestige offers. But one day your country is invaded and you are captured. You are taken to a foreign land as a slave—stripped of your family, honor, wealth and religion. What would you do? How would you react?

That is the position that Daniel, the man we think of as a hero and a prophet, found himself in. What is significant that you may not know is that this happened to Daniel when he was only seventeen years old! A teenager—who was of royal descent—now a slave among strangers!

The Bible tells us Daniel was taken prisoner by King Nebuchadnezzar of Babylon who besieged the city of Jerusalem (Daniel 1:1). Think of the horrors of war he must have seen, the terror he must have felt when his city, his people, his family were destroyed before his eyes. When Daniel was dragged off to Babylon, he had one consolation—he was not alone. He had three friends with him—other princes the Bible says—and of course Daniel had God.

Hananiah, Mishael and Azariah were also children of Judah taken captive along with Daniel. You may know them as Shadrach, Meshack and Abnego. Their names were changed by the eunuch in charge of them. Daniel became Belteshazzar. Imagine how that must have felt. Now you have lost everything—even your name!

But there was something special about Daniel and his friends. Though they may have looked like average kids, they were not. Today they would have been the kids running the Beta club, the Honor Society, and the Student Council. We know this because the Bible says the king told his head over the eunuchs to pick out the best of the children from Israel, the ones who were "skillful in wisdom," "cunning in knowledge," who were "understanding in science" without a blemish and who had the ability to serve in the king's palace (Daniel 1:4). In addition to that, they had to be smart enough to learn the Chaldean language. A mighty tall order! The king gave the head eunuch three years to train, teach and generally whip these young guys into shape. At the end of that time, the king expected them to be able to stand before him and serve in his palace (verse 5).

In an effort to change the loyalty of these young Jewish captives, not only are their names changed, not only are they put through an extensive training program in Babylonian education and culture, but they are given the best food the king can offer. This is the way foreign invaders yet today assimilate captives into their society.

However, there was just one thing that stood in the way of making Babylonians out of these Jewish youths—and that was Jehovah God. It might have been just one thing, but when that one thing is God—that's a big thing!

Though Daniel was cooperative when he could be, Daniel and his three friends determined, resolved to be faithful to God. They "purposed in their heart." That means they thought about it and made a deliberate decision (verse 8).

When the eunuch wanted them to eat of the king's food and drink his wine, Daniel asked him to allow them not to. Notice how Daniel did not act out of rebellion but out of conviction. Daniel's request was made respectfully to the eunuch, and most importantly, out of respect for God's law. He would not defile himself by eating the king's food (verse 8). How many ways do young people defile themselves today?

The eunuch made a deal with Daniel. If he and his friends were still healthy after eating pulse (vegetables) and drinking water for ten days, then he would continue to allow it. Daniel and his friends proved to be quite healthy, and for standing by God's law they were blessed by God. He rewarded their faith by giving them wisdom and skill in learning. God especially blessed Daniel with the gift of interpreting dreams and visions (1:17), but all four boys were so blessed with understanding and wisdom that the king himself recognized them as ten times better than all the magicians and enchanters in his kingdom!

Daniel goes on to become a great man in Babylon. He uses the gift God gave him to save lives and to glorify God. Daniel became the third most powerful man in all Babylon, it is true; however, he never left the One whom he knew power came from. Daniel's trust in God and His way was deep in his heart as a young man, so we are not surprised that in Daniel's old age we find him in a den of lions because he would not stop praying to God. As always, God was with Daniel (Daniel chapter 6).

Today God will be with us as well. But we must do what Daniel did. We must be true to God: 1) even if our family is not with us; 2) even if someone older demands otherwise; and 3) even when things are hard. Daniel was a strong and faithful teenager; you can be too!

LESSONS FROM DANIEL:

In Work—Daniel worked for a king, in fact several, who were not of his religion, culture, or ethnic background. This did not stop him from hard work and even advancement.

In Worship—Daniel did not allow even a king to stop him from worshipping his God. He worshipped regularly too.

In Life—The Bible says Daniel had an excellent spirit. This handsome young man was handsome in heart as well. Also notice, he made friends with the faithful. It was Daniel's three friends who later refused to bow to the image of the king. For their loyalty to God they were thrown into a fiery furnace. But the Son of God delivered them unharmed (Daniel 3). These brave young men were worthy of Daniel's friendship.

In Home—Daniel was snatched away from his home but he never forgot the values he was taught there. Parents strive to teach their children in such a way that when they are away from them their children continue to do what's right. Daniel's parents would have been proud of how he continued to live out his heritage of righteousness.

DISCUSSION:

1. Name three ways young people defile themselves today.

2. Why didn't Daniel blame God for being taken into captivity?

3. What was it about Daniel that won over the head eunuch?

4. Name a time you were not true to God. What would you do differently now? What would Daniel have done in your situation?

LESSON 2

Joseph

Have you ever been mistreated by someone in your family, maybe by one of your brothers or sisters? What would you do if you had ten brothers and they all hated you? They hated you so much they wanted to kill you but instead threw you in a pit and then sold you into slavery, expecting, hoping to never see you again?

That is the hatred and jealousy felt by the brothers of Joseph, son of Jacob. Joseph was his father's favorite. Maybe this was true because Joseph was born when Jacob was 91 years old, or maybe Joseph was his favorite because Joseph was the son of Rachel, Jacob's favorite wife, the one the Bible says Jacob loved. But most especially, Joseph was favored because of his goodness of character.

Joseph's goodness didn't matter to his brothers though. In fact, sometimes when you are good it makes people hate you even more. Such was the case with Joseph's brothers. Add to that that their father gave Joseph a special coat "of many colors" (Genesis 37:2). The icing on the cake was that Joseph had dreams, dreams that indicated his brothers would bow down to him someday. This totaled up to a horrible hatred, a gigantic jealousy.

Joseph's brothers proceed to sell him for 20 pieces of silver. They would've killed him had it not been for Reuben, his oldest brother. Seventeen years old and his family is gone. Strangers (Ishmaelites) take him to a foreign land (Egypt). How do you think Joseph felt? Angry? Hurt? Afraid? Surely he was all those things. It's only natural;

however, Joseph does not let these feelings remain within him to rule his life. He does not become bitter or filled with self pity. He does not allow life's adversity to change who he is. He may be a slave instead of the favored son but that didn't change who Joseph was on the inside.

Hatred almost always leads to other sins. Hating Joseph leads his brothers to lie to their father. They lead him to believe Joseph has been killed by a wild animal. Jacob grieves so that the Bible says he could not be comforted. But Joseph doesn't know that his father thinks he's dead. Consider how Joseph must have felt when his father did not come to find him. He must have had a broken heart for some time.

This sad teenager was next sold to a man named Potiphar who was one of Pharaoh's officers in Egypt. It is evident that Joseph came to terms with his bad situation. He accepted it and made the best of it. "And the Lord was with Joseph, and he was a prosperous man" (Genesis 39:2). Joseph was successful. Potiphar even noticed it. Everything in Joseph's hand prospered. So Potiphar put Joseph over all his house. What a happy ending to a terrific story! But that's not the end.

Joseph's life is shaped by lies, the lie of his brothers and the lie of a woman. Potiphar's wife tries to seduce Joseph, not just once but day after day the text says. Joseph's response is "How can I do this great wickedness, and sin against God?" (Genesis 39:9). When he won't lie with her, she lies to her husband about Joseph and Potiphar puts Joseph in prison.

Through all of the injustices experienced by Joseph, he reacted righteously. Genesis 39:21-23 says, "But the Lord was with Joseph and showed him mercy, and He gave him favor in the sight of the keeper of the prison. And the keeper of the prison committed to Joseph's hand all the prisoners who were in the prison; whatever they did there, it was his doing. The keeper of the prison did not look into anything that was under Joseph's authority, because the Lord was with him; and whatever he did, the Lord made it prosper."

Joseph spent two years in the king's prison. During that time he interpreted dreams for the king's chief butler and baker who had been thrown in prison as well. When the butler was released he forgot about Joseph...until a special day. Pharaoh was having dreams that none of his magicians could interpret. Finally the butler remembered...Joseph!

When they called for Joseph to come to Pharaoh, king of Egypt, Joseph hurried to him. But the Bible says he first shaved and changed his clothes. Joseph was wise; he recognized an opportunity and endeavored to put his best foot forward. Joseph of course successfully interprets Pharaoh's dreams, giving God all the glory, and everything Joseph says comes true. Pharaoh rewards Joseph with clothing, jewelry, a wife and power over his land. Joseph is no longer a sad teenaged slave but a prosperous man of 30 by now!

We all know the story of how Joseph's brothers end up coming to Egypt for food during the famine. They don't recognize their brother. He's a grown man now wearing Egyptian clothing and speaking to them through an interpreter. Joseph tests his brothers' integrity by putting money in their sacks. They return that which is not theirs and also follow all of Joseph's instructions.

When Joseph finally reveals himself to his brethren he weeps loudly, telling them not to be grieved or angry with themselves because God had sent him to Egypt to preserve life, that God had sent him to save their lives and God had made him lord over all Egypt. Joseph has grown up into such a mature man, hasn't he? Not bitter or vengeful but meekly and courageously accepting the providence of God in his life.

LESSONS FROM JOSEPH:

In Work—Joseph, like Daniel, worked for a king and king's officer who were foreign to him. Yet, because of his honest diligence, God blessed him with advancement, prosperity, and prestige.

In Worship—Joseph recognized and praised God throughout his life. He knew where his gifts came from and Who was responsible for how his life was blessed.

In Life—Joseph never hardened his heart, no matter how awful the lie or action done against him. He remained tenderhearted and forgiving (note the number of times he wept while dealing with his brothers and finally his father—Genesis 47-50).

In Home—Like Daniel, Joseph never forgot his family heritage. After reuniting with his father, he provided for him in Egypt until Jacob died (Genesis 47:11, 27-28).

DISCUSSION:

1. Read 2 Timothy 2:22. How does this verse reflect Joseph's life? How is it reflected in your own?

2. How did God bless Joseph even when he was in prison?

3. Name two or three things that happened to Joseph that prove God was working out His will in Joseph's life.

4. Do you believe God is working providentially in your life? (Hebrews 13:5; Ephesians 3:20-21) We don't know specifically in our own lives what God is doing. We know specifically about Joseph because God has revealed it. However, we must, like Joseph, choose to live righteously no matter what events occur.

5. What did Joseph do concerning the seven years of plenty and seven years of famine that showed his wisdom? (Genesis 41)

LESSON 3

Timothy

We don't know how old Timothy was exactly when he met the apostle Paul, the man who would change his life. But we do know he was young when he obeyed the gospel because of Paul's exhortations to him as a "youth."

Timothy was raised in a "mixed" family—his mother was a Jewess and his father was Greek. This surely caused conflicts; however his mother and grandmother did not let this deter them from teaching Timothy the Holy Scriptures. He knew them from childhood (2 Timothy 1:5). How many of us have at least one parent or grandparent that is faithful to God but we pay no attention to their knowledge or teaching of God's word? Timothy was not guilty of this. He had a spirit, a heart open to the teaching of his mother and grandmother.

Paul converted Timothy on his first missionary journey. Timothy learned his devotion and zeal from this great apostle. He "fully" knew —witnessed—Paul's persecutions (2 Timothy 3:10-17). To see with your own eyes the kind of unflinching faith that would carry a man through beatings, stoning, all manner of mistreatments—this was a lesson in love that Timothy would take to his grave. Who is your example? Who are you watching, spending your time with, learning from? Timothy chose to be Paul's helper; he didn't have to leave Lystra, but he did. He saw the Lord in Paul and he wanted to help in any way he could. We have great Christians today, men and women, whose life examples should inspire you to stronger faith and more work in God's kingdom, the church. Take notice of them. Learn from them. Appreciate them.

Not only did Timothy appreciate Paul but Paul had a special regard for Timothy as well. He called him his "dearly beloved son," remembered him in his "prayers night and day" and "greatly desired" to see him when they were separated. But more than affection, Paul had much respect for and trust in Timothy. When he wrote the Philippians, Paul told them he would send Timothy to them, that no one was as like-minded as he to care for them (Philippians 2:19-22). What a compliment to Timothy! Their trust was also mutual. Timothy allowed Paul to circumcise him when Paul deemed it necessary for the work (Acts 16:3). How many of you young men trust someone that much?

Paul's trust and regard for Timothy is seen in the responsibilities he charged him with. Timothy traveled with Paul to many cities, was involved in constant mission work, but he also remained in Ephesus alone for some time. It was here in Ephesus that Timothy was charged with seeing to it that no one teach false doctrine (1 Timothy 1:3). What a great and difficult job for a young man. He was to make sure elders were qualified, that worship was conducted properly, that the widows were cared for, that the women were acting (and dressing) right, along with the slaves, rich, etc! Just imagine the pressure on this young man! Who was going to listen to him anyway?! He was a kid, a new convert himself, what did he know?! 1 Timothy 4:12 lets us know that Paul was well aware of Timothy's youth and that he would have trouble commanding respect from his elders. He told him how to gain that respect, by setting an example in his speech, conduct, love, faith and purity. There is a liability of youth that all of us must endure. Many older people don't expect youth to have any sense or maturity about them. Timothy experienced this as well. Oddly enough, sometimes it is the young people who have the passion for the truth and fervent love for the Lord that the older folks have lost. Timothy is an example of this.

It was not only in Ephesus that Timothy encountered conflict as a young person. According to 1 Corinthians 16:10-11, we might conclude that the Corinthians also were not welcoming to Timothy. Though Timothy delivered this epistle for Paul and lived in Corinth for probably two years at least, it's interesting to note that Titus delivered the second epistle to the Corinthians, not Timothy. It is a difficult lesson to learn in life—that not everyone will accept you—that sometimes you must step aside and let someone else do the job for the benefit of the most good. This is what Timothy did. It is encouraging to know, however, that Luke tells us Timothy was well spoken of and "highly esteemed" by his brethren in Lystra and Iconium (Acts 16:2). This speaks volumes for Timothy, especially since Lystra was his hometown.

LESSONS FROM TIMOTHY:

In Work—Tradition says Timothy became an elder at Ephesus. We know for certain that Timothy abounded in the work of the Lord.

In Worship—Paul gave specific commands to Timothy about worship. It was a part of his job at Ephesus to see that the public worship to God was done according to truth (1 Timothy 1:3; 3:15). Do you know enough of God's word to be sure you are worshipping properly? Or are you just following your parents?

In Life—Timothy was young like you; that means he endured the same temptations. He had to apply Paul's admonitions to his life, just like you do. Secular history says Timothy died a martyr under Domitian. It is not likely God will require this of you, but He does require you to live for Him!

In Home—Timothy heeded the teachings of his mother and grandmother. He respected them (those teaching him and what they taught). He must have lived out this respect at home as a loving, dutiful son for this was the type of young man Paul found and converted to the Lord.

DISCUSSION:

1. Are you esteemed highly by other Christians?

2. Paul admonished Timothy to keep himself pure (1 Timothy 5:22; 2 Timothy 2:22) and flee youthful lusts. Are you doing that? What can young people do to help accomplish this?

3. Timothy had great responsibility in the church. It is true his work was unique in helping the early church begin. However, all Christians have responsibilities in the kingdom. What do you see as yours (generally and specifically)? Find something specific that you can do in the church. Go to an elder and ask for a job if you don't know of one. How truly they would esteem you for your attitude and help.

4. Was Timothy ever imprisoned for his belief? (Consider Hebrews 13:23.)

5. Name someone in the church who you esteem, someone you look to as an example. How are they an influence on you? Can you be that kind of influence for someone else?

LESSON 4

David

He was a shepherd, a warrior and a king. He was also an adulterer and murderer, yet through it all—a child of God whom God Himself would say was after His heart (Acts 13:22). What an amazing and special individual was David, son of Jesse.

The story we know best of David, the one we sang about as children, is of course about how he killed Goliath. David was seventeen years old on that day—only 17! Think about it. The youngest of ten, his job was watching his father's sheep. His brothers were at war against the Philistines when David's father told him to take them food at their encampment. It was there that David heard Goliath blaspheme the God of the Israelites. We all know the outcome, how David only needed one of his five smooth stones to bring Goliath down. But there may be a point or two we've overlooked. David's oldest brother Eliab rebuked David for coming to the battlefield. Saul also tried to discourage David by saying, "You're just a youth; Goliath's a man of war." Can you imagine how the Israelites must have laughed at him? Goliath had been defying them for 40 days (morning and night) and now this kid comes along and thinks he can do better?! Yet with all the hindrances, David let nothing stop him. David's faith was greater than all that day. He said, God was with me when I killed a lion and bear; he'll be with me when I kill this Philistine. He drew near to Goliath and boldly declared, "Thou comest to me with a sword and with a spear; and with a shield; but I come to thee in the name of the Lord of hosts, the God of the armies of Israel, whom thou hast defied. This day will the Lord deliver thee into mine hand; and I will smite thee, and take thine head from thee; and I will give the carcasses of the host of the Philistines this day unto the fowls of the air, and to the wild beasts of the earth; that all the earth may know that there is a God in Israel. And all this assembly shall know that the Lord saveth not with sword and spear: for the battle is the Lord's, and he will give you into our hands" (1 Samuel 17:45-47). And amazingly verse 48 tells us David "hasted"—hurried—toward the Philistine army to meet Goliath. He ran straight into the enemy army! What kind of teenager was this?! One like you. No? You can be a David. Begin now to develop that kind of faith—the kind of faith that can topple giants.

The same day David killed Goliath David acquired his best friend —Jonathan. Jonathan saw what David had done, his faith, his courage. Some might have been jealous but not Jonathan. Even though Jonathan was the king's son and was probably 10 to 15 years older than David, his was genuine admiration and love for his young friend. From that day forward their souls were "knit" together (1 Samuel 18:1-3). Their similar qualities produced mutual love, and Jonathan helped David reach his full potential. That's what true friendships do, and that's why they are sacred, precious, and worth risking your life over. This is exactly what Jonathan did for David.

The day of David's victory over Goliath began David's career as a soldier. Since God was with David, David was successful and grew mightily as a warrior. Saul appointed him as captain over 1,000 men. As his success grew, so did his popularity. The Bible says, "But all Is-rael and Judah loved David, because he went out and came in before them" (1 Samuel 18:16). He was accepted by all the people and even Saul's servants (1 Samuel 18:5). But as is often the case, popularity brings jealousy. When the people sing higher praise to David than they do to Saul, scripture says, "Saul eyed David from that day and forward" (1 Samuel 18:9). That was the beginning of the end—the end of David's relationship with the king and the end of Saul's king-ship.

One of the truly amazing things about David is popularity didn't spoil him. David "behaved himself wisely in all his ways," "very wise-ly" the text repeats (1 Samuel 18:14-15). He never was conceited, and he always acted humbly so as not to cause jealousy when he was pro-moted. Jonathan loved him for it (his heart was right) while Saul hat-ed him (his heart was not right) so Saul became his "enemy continu-ally."

Eventually David had to run for his life. But he remained loyal to Saul even when Saul continued to try to kill him. David had oppor-tunity to kill Saul on more than one occasion but he didn't (1 Samuel 24:10; 26:11). Saul, on the other hand, even killed the Lord's priests to try to get to David (1 Samuel 23:21). We learn, sadly, that hatred will kill you. Saul is mortally wounded by the Philistines, along with three of his sons—yes, even Jonathan. Imagine David's broken heart! Read his words of anguish and grief in 2 Samuel chapter 1.

At 30 years of age David is anointed king (2 Samuel 5:4). The tri-als and threats he suffered in his early life served to bring David strength for tasks in his later life.

Though we remember David's faith, his courage, his loyalty—David was not a perfect man. He was very real. He fell to temptation of the flesh as so many of us have. David saw a woman (Bathsheba) bathing one day and he had to have her. He became so obsessed that he sent her husband to the frontlines of battle to be killed so he could legally have her. Here the Bible teaches us that we sin when we use someone else's hands to commit a crime for us. Thus, David becomes a murderer (2 Samuel 11-12).

Fortunately, David had a friend who was courageous and compassionate enough to rebuke a king. Nathan cared for David's soul and stood up to David. "Thou art the man" (2 Samuel 12:7). It is fortunate as well that David had an honest heart. When confronted with the truth about himself, David repented and turned back to God. This is why David was said to be a man after God's heart. He always turned back to God in tears and contrition (Psalm 51).

David's life was not all sweetness and light. He endured much, some consequences of his own actions, some from others. He suffered the death of his baby as punishment for his adultery with Bathsheba. Later his daughter Tamar was raped by her half-brother. His eldest son Amnon was murdered. His favorite son Absalom revolted against him and later was accidentally killed. David's heart was broken over and over again. Once in the midst of his battles two of David's wives were taken captive. He found and saved them of course! After all, he was God's warrior-king!

At the end of his eventful life, David's son Solomon is crowned king. David gives Solomon these final instructions: "I go the way of all the earth: be thou strong therefore, and shew thyself a man; and keep the charge of the Lord thy God, to walk in his ways, to keep his statutes, and his commandments, and his judgments, and his testimonies, as it is written in the law of Moses, that thou mayest prosper in all that thou doest, and whithersoever thou turnest thyself; that the Lord may continue his word which he spake concerning me, saying, If thy children take heed to their way, to walk before me in truth with all their heart and with all their soul, there shall not fail thee (said he) a man on the throne of Israel" (I Kings 2:2-4).

From a handsome 17-year-old with auburn hair and sparkling eyes (1 Samuel 16:12) to a bearded 70-year-old man who could not keep warm (1 Kings 1:1), David teaches us about courage, faith, and loyalty for that is what he lived.

LESSONS FROM DAVID:

In Work—David took his work seriously all of his life. As a boy/teenager, he protected sheep, fed them and cared for them. He used his genius at music and poetry to sing and play for the king. He battled with great strength even into old age. Never do we see David become lazy or uncaring in any job.

In Worship—David praised God his entire life. He gave God the glory for every deliverance in battle. We have the Psalms, most of which are David's beautiful praise poetry. David also was sacrificial in his worship. He said, "Nay; but I will surely buy it of thee at a price: neither will I offer burnt offerings unto the Lord my God of that which doth cost me nothing" (2 Samuel 24:24). In 1 Chronicles 13 we see David bring the ark of the covenant back to Jerusalem where it was supposed to be. He loved God so much that he wanted the ark to be in God's designated place.

In Life—Most of the time when David was in danger he cast his cares upon God. But, like us, David could forget Who was by his side. He cried out that there was but a step between him and death (1 Samuel 20:3), forgetting God would protect him from Saul. We must never forget Who is by our side.

David also greatly teaches us about friendship. He and Jonathan made a vow, a promise to each other (1 Samuel 20:16-17). What do vows mean to you? David kept his—even after Jonathan's death, by caring for Jonathan's son, Mephibosheth (2 Samuel 9:13). How precious are your friends to you?

In Home—David obeyed his father. He was an obedient shepherd and messenger as a youth. David heeded the lessons of God's word that were taught to him and carried that faith with him until he died.

DISCUSSION:

1. David stood up for God to a 9 foot tall Philistine. Have you ever stood up for God to anyone?

2. Saul was jealous of David. Are you guilty of that sin? How can you learn to rejoice for others who are successful or when they receive praise?

3. What sin of David's led to other sins?

4. Read 2 Samuel 12:1-3 again. Do you have a friend like Nathan who will tell you the truth? Are you a friend like that to someone? Read David's response in verse 13. Are you humble when your sins are pointed out or are you stubborn, defensive, or plain blind?

5. Read David's praise in 2 Samuel 22:20-51. Can you say verses 22-25? What needs to be changed so you can?

LESSON 5

Josiah

Isn't it amazing how sometimes good kids can come from really bad homes? Though rare, we've all seen it. This is what happened to Josiah. His grandfather Manasseh was wicked (2 Kings 21:1-2) and his father Amon was wicked (2 Kings 21:20). Amon was so evil his own servants killed him (2 Kings 21:23). Then along comes little Josiah. He was eight years old when he became king. King of Judah—a daunting task for an eight year old! But, in spite of being reared by an evil father, in spite of his youth, the Bible says Josiah "did that which was right in the sight of the Lord, and walked in all the ways of David his father, and turned not aside to the right hand or to the left" (2 Kings 22:2). Maybe Josiah's mother, Jedidah, taught her son the ways of the Lord. Maybe he was taught about the life of King David. We don't know, but there is no doubt Josiah chose a different path from his father for when he was 16 "in the eighth year of his reign, while he was yet young, he began to seek after the God of David his father; and in the twelfth year he began to purge Judah and Jerusalem from the high places, and the groves, and the carved images, and the molten images" (2 Chronicles 34:3).

In Josiah's 18th year he decided the house of the Lord was in need of repair. He wanted the carpenters, masons and builders to "repair the breaches of the house." This was a noble cause and reflects Josiah's good heart. This, however, was just the beginning of the good works of this young man for God.

When the priest Hilkiah gathered the money from the temple for the repairs, he found a book. It was God's book.

Josiah's scribe Shaphan read the book—the law of Moses—to the king and Josiah rent his clothes. Why was he upset? Because he discovered that he and his people were not following all of God's laws. Through the prophetess Huldah, God told Josiah "Because thine heart was tender, and thou hast humbled thyself before the Lord, when thou heardest what I spake against this place, and against the inhabitants thereof, that they should become a desolation and a curse, and hast rent thy clothes, and wept before me; I also have heard thee, saith the Lord. Behold therefore, I will gather thee unto thy fathers, and thou shalt be gathered into thy grave in peace; and thine eyes shall not see all the evil which I bring upon this place. And they brought the king word again" (2 Kings 22:19-20).

For the first time in many years the Passover was kept by the people at the command of King Josiah.

There were many in Judah, however, that did not worship the God of heaven. Idolatry was commonplace. But when Josiah learned of God's will, he did not sit idly by and allow his people to be an abomination. He commanded "to bring forth...and he burned them..." (2 Kings 23:4). He broke down all the idols and stamped them to dust. He shut down the valley where idolaters sacrificed their children to Molech. He broke down the houses of the sodomites (homosexuals) and he killed the priests of the idols and burned them upon their own altars. Does it sound like Josiah meant business?! The Bible further says Josiah put away the workers with familiar spirits, wizards, images, idols and all abominations in the land of Judah "...that he might perform the words of the law which were written in the book..." (2 Kings 23:24). What an incredible young man! No one had ever done anything like this before and no one did afterward.

Josiah's life ended when he was only 39 years old. He was killed in a battle with the king of Egypt at Megiddo. His servants brought him in a chariot to Jerusalem where he was buried in his own sepulcher.

The child-king Josiah was like no other. God says so. "And like unto him was there no king before him, that turned to the Lord with all his heart, and with all his soul, and with all his might, according to all the law of Moses; neither after him arose there any like him" (2 Kings 23:25).

LESSONS FROM JOSIAH:

In Work—Josiah took seriously his job as ruler of Judah. He put forth every effort to save his people.

In Worship—2 Chronicles 34:31 tells us Josiah made a covenant with the Lord, "to walk after him…" He read the word of the Lord to the people himself, all the people, including the Levites, priests, all great and small. Josiah expected everyone to come to the house of the Lord and to attend to the words of the book. Not only did he expect it —he caused all to "stand to it." It was Josiah's desire that God receive His due praise and adoration. As their leader, Josiah saw to it that this was done. Where are such leaders today?

Another point of interest—when Josiah "found" God's word, did he say Israel hasn't followed these laws for decades, why start now. No, Josiah recognized the passing of time did not change God's law, His truth or what was right. The same is true today. No matter how long your Bible has been in the dust on the shelf, you can pick it up, read it and begin to obey it. You can change your life and become pleasing to God, leaving a legacy like Josiah.

In Life—One of the sweetest lessons of Josiah is how a young heart can be pricked. His tender heart brought him to immediate repentance when he learned the truth which resulted in immediate action. Can you say the same for yourself? When you heard the gospel, how did you respond? Were you disturbed and humbled like Josiah? Did you take immediate action like he did to make things right with God?

Another lesson Josiah teaches us is that our environment is no excuse for doing wrong. Josiah's father was horribly wicked but Josiah did not let his parents, environment, his power or wealth stop him from making his own clear choice for God and righteousness.

In Home—Josiah's home life probably wasn't a good one. Yet he rises above the evil of his father, even as a teenager, and becomes one of the greatest kings God ever blessed. When our home life is not what it should be, we can remember faithful Josiah who "turned not aside to the right hand or the left" but followed the Lord.

DISCUSSION:

1. Who aided Josiah in the spreading of the knowledge of God and lamented at his death? (2 Chronicles 35:25)

2. Read 2 Chronicles 35:26. What acts of goodness did he do? Is this how we define goodness today?

3. How do you account for Josiah's good heart and seeking God when he was 16 though he had such a wicked family?

4. Do we respect the reading of the word of God the way Josiah did? Do we worship regularly with true devotion? What does reverence really mean? Is this a Sunday attitude or day-to-day attitude?

LESSON 6

Esther

She was an orphan. She was just a young girl. She was a captive Jew in a foreign land. And worst of all, she was beautiful. How can that be a bad thing you ask? When a wicked king wants to replace his queen, being beautiful is not a plus for a sweet young girl. But this exceptional girl turned her beauty to her advantage and used it for God's cause.

Her name was Hadassah; we know her as Esther. Though an orphan, Esther was fortunate to be raised by her Uncle Mordecai, a godly man who would bow to no one but Jehovah.

When King Ahaseurus was disrespected by Queen Vashti, he began a search for a new queen. King Ahaseurus is one of history's most wicked rulers. He did not set up interviews for this position. He commanded that his chamberlain arrange their preparation (Esther 2:2-4) and then one by one he physically "took" these girls to find one who satisfied him best. This is what happened to poor Esther. Raped by a man, an evil man probably much older than she was, who had the power to have her killed. We wonder how she endured it. She not only managed to live through the ordeal, however; she found the strength within herself to act in such a way that the king was impressed with her. She found favor with him, not only because she was beautiful but because she was gracious.

A brave and intelligent young girl, Esther also was loyal. After being chosen queen, she happened to learn of a plan to kill the king

(Esther 2:22-23). She did not rejoice in that evil but instead told the king of the murderous plot. You can imagine his gratitude and also the trust this created in the king for Esther.

Ahaseurus' top prince was named Haman. Haman also was a wicked man. Because of his wounded pride, Haman concocted a plan to ensure the death of Mordecai when Mordecai would not bow to Haman. Haman knew Mordecai was a Jew (but he didn't know Esther was his niece). So Haman convinced the king to decree that the Jews be killed.

Who could save the Jewish nation from utter destruction? Who could ensure the Messiah would still be born? A beautiful young girl named Esther. Haman had a plan but so did God!

Mordecai told Esther "who knows but that you've come to the kingdom for such a time as this" (Esther 4:14). She had a decision to make. If she went to court to speak to the king without being summoned, she could lose her life. She fasts, prays and asks Mordecai to ask everyone else to do so as well. Then she says with courage, "if I perish, I perish" (vs. 16).

Esther took action. She went to the king. She did not wait for someone else to do the job. She did not sit down and wait to die. She heroically faced the challenge and God blessed her. Her plan became God's plan because she did what was right—even when it was hard.

Because of Esther the Jews were saved and Haman got what he deserved. God used a beautiful young girl to accomplish His will. Do you believe He can use you too? This is how great our God is. He can take our marred clay and still make beautiful vessels out of it. We must allow Him to transform us into heroes, like Esther, by obeying Him, growing in courage and facing life's challenges.

LESSONS FROM ESTHER:

In Work—Esther was a loyal queen who served her king. She acted appropriately in her position and found favor with everyone (Esther 2:15).

In Worship—Fasting and prayer were a part of Esther's life. She depended on the God of heaven. No doubt Mordecai had taught Esther to worship God regularly.

In Life—Esther made the best of a bad situation. She didn't run away or bury her head in the sand. She did not live in a perpetual pity party either, crying "oh poor me, look what's happened to me!" She dealt with her troubles the way we all should, smiling (finding favor with others) and on our knees (finding favor with God).

In Home—Mordecai raised a brave girl. His faith was reflected in her. He taught her God's providence was real and encouraged her to let God use her for the good. Esther did not whine and say, "I have no parents" and use that as an excuse to do wrong. Instead she rejoiced in the love of a kind relative.

DISCUSSION:

1. Have you ever done something good for a very wicked person like Esther did?

2. Do you pray and/or fast before making a decision like Esther did? Have you ever fasted? What is the value of it? Is prayer a habit of your spiritual life?

3. Analyze the verses Galatians 6:7-8 in light of Haman.

4. Are you using your beauty or other positive attributes for God's cause? How?

5. Has anything bad ever happened to you that may be similar to Esther being taken by the king? Hurt or violated by someone? Have you let that incident define the rest of your life or have you risen above it? Can you "press forward" (Philippians 3:12-13) and re-write the script of your life?

LESSON 7

The Israelite Maid

She was a slave. She had lived through war and had been taken captive by the Syrians. The scriptures refer to her as "a little maid" but what great big lessons she teaches us!

She was a servant in an important household. She "waited on Naaman's wife." Naaman was captain of the host of the king of Syria. He was a mighty man of valor. He had delivered his country. He had done great things but he had a great problem. He was a leper.

The little maid spoke up to her mistress. She had mercy and said, "Would God my lord were with the prophet that is in Samaria! For he would recover him of his leprosy" (2 Kings 5:3). She could have been bitter, spiteful, and selfish but no—she shared the knowledge of God's prophet.

Next, look at her faith. She had no doubt Naaman could be healed of his leprosy. She *knew* (true belief) that God's prophet could help him. Mercy and trust—a beautiful combination that God will always bless. The maiden did not hide the knowledge of God as we do sometimes; she did not fear the captain either. A brave and faithful girl who brought salvation to a stranger!—and because of her, Naaman spoke these amazing words, "Behold, now I know that there is no God in all the earth, but in Israel…" (2 Kings 5:15).

LESSONS FROM THE MAID:

In Work—She was a servant who cared about her captors.

In Worship—She had not lost her faith in the foreign land. She knew God's prophet; she knew God.

In Life—Like Esther, this maiden made the best of a bad situation. She was a slave who did her job and continued to hold on to a caring heart.

In Home—Her own home was gone; she lived in Naaman's household. We know nothing of her parents or family. They may have been killed in the war or they were just separated from one another. Whichever, we know she came from a home of faith.

DISCUSSION:

1. Why was Naaman upset with God's prophet?

2. What was the result of the maid sharing the knowledge of God's prophet?

3. Do you think she rejoiced in his cleansing?

4. Have you ever told anyone how to be "cleansed"?

John Mark

John Mark is the writer of the second gospel account. Tradition says Peter related the events Mark wrote, but we know he was inspired of God (2 Peter 1:21). He lived in Jerusalem. His mother allowed the church to meet in her house. It was there, at Mark's home, where the Christians prayed for Peter to be released from prison (Acts 12:12).

Mark went with Paul and Barnabas to Cyprus on Paul's first missionary journey. This trip proved to be a problem for all of them. Mark decided halfway through while in Perga in Pamphylia to leave and go back home (Acts 13:13). The Bible doesn't tell us why. He may have been homesick or afraid. He was young; maybe this was the first time he was away from home. He could have been lonely there with two older men. Or possibly their safety had been threatened. Christians were being persecuted everywhere. Then again, he could have had a personal conflict with Barnabas (who happened to be his uncle) or with the apostle Paul. Whatever the reason, Mark says I'm outta here!

The Bible does tell us that later when Paul and Barnabas set out again Paul refused to take Mark with them. This caused such a contention between Barnabas and Paul that they separated. Mark went with Barnabas to Cyprus while Paul took Silas to Syria and Cilicia (Acts 15:36-41). On the surface this sounds bad, doesn't it? But amazingly enough, later Paul writes to Timothy to bring Mark to him in Rome because he would be profitable to him in his ministry (2 Timothy 4:11). What? Something changed, didn't it? Was it Paul's attitude or was it Mark's? We don't know for sure, maybe both. But we do know that Mark became a loyal friend and helper to Paul despite their once sharp separation.

LESSONS FROM MARK:

In Work—Don't allow criticism to keep you from doing the Lord's work. If you do what is right, you will earn people's respect. Small start—big end!

In Worship—John Mark had a mother who was devoted and taught her son. Peter came to their house where they were praying for him.

In Life—John Mark shows us how you can develop from an apprehensive young person to a "fellow laborer" alongside great mature Christians.

In Home—Home was important to Mark because apparently that's where he ran back to. Perhaps he was homesick and missing his family. Whatever the reason, we know his home is where Christians met, and that is where he wanted to be.

DISCUSSION:

1. Reread Acts 13 and 15. Why do you think John Mark left Paul and Barnabas?

2. If Mark was afraid because of persecution he witnessed, what changed his mind?

3. How do we know Barnabas had a great influence on Mark?

4. How do you react to criticism? If someone tried to stop you from doing the Lord's work, what would you do?

LESSON 9

Paul's Nephew

Would you like to do something to change history? Have you ever saved anyone's life? I know someone who has done both—a young man whose name is a secret to us—the Apostle Paul's nephew.

Paul had been making a defense in front of the Jewish council. The Sadducees and Pharisees began to argue with Paul and each other. The chief captain had soldiers take Paul by force and put him inside the castle to protect him.

A group of Jews vowed to kill Paul. In fact, they vowed not to eat or drink until he was dead. Somehow Paul's nephew overheard these Jews making their deadly plans. What do you think he did? Ignore it, say hey I'm just a kid, what can I do? No, he went to his Uncle Paul and told him what he had heard the wicked men planning. Do you imagine that took some courage? Truly it did because that probably meant he had to sneak into the castle and find Paul who was being guarded. When he told his uncle what he had heard, Paul told a centurion to take his nephew to the chief captain. His nephew told the chief captain about the Jews' plan and thankfully the captain believed him. He sent him on his way, admonishing him not to tell anyone else.

Because Paul's nephew had courage and great love for his uncle, the Apostle Paul was saved from certain death (Acts 23:11-35). This young man teaches us several valuable lessons: 1) Take action when it is needed, no matter your age. 2) Love carries responsibility with it. 3)

You can make a difference, a big difference, even if it is only to one person. Paul's nephew took action. He did not say no one is going to listen to me, how can I get to my uncle, they may arrest me too—no excuses; he acted. This young man's love for his uncle meant he took the responsibility for Paul's welfare; he truly loved as he should. And finally, this young man made a big difference in Paul's life, didn't he? He not only saved Paul's life—by saving Paul, he probably saved many others in a more important way—by the saving of their souls through Paul's preaching!

LESSONS FROM PAUL'S NEPHEW:

In Home—Paul's nephew was raised by Jewish parents who had taught him a great love for family. This was exhibited in his actions taken for his uncle.

In Work—We have no record of Paul's nephew anywhere else other than this chapter in Acts 23, but we can believe that this young man grew up to be a man of responsibility and action.

In Life—Paul's nephew is a lesson for us in love, courage, and character, so we know these things must have been the habit of his life.

In Worship—We do not know if Paul's nephew was a Christian, but we do know his uncle no doubt had taught him the gospel. Paul's nephew was a Jew so we know he was raised believing in the God of heaven surely taught by Paul's sister and her husband.

DISCUSSION:

1. Have you ever done something that exhibited bravery? Ever saved anybody?

2. Has anyone ever saved your life? For what purpose were you saved—maybe to do something great for others like Paul?

3. How would history have changed if Paul's nephew had not taken action?

4. What does age have to do with courage?

5. Can you be brave and still be afraid?

LESSON 10

Jesus

In case you didn't realize it, your Savior was a teenager once! Yes, He was. He had an earthly father and mother just like you do. In all probability He grew up in His father Joseph's carpenter shop, learning his trade as was the custom. Jesus had brothers and sisters (Matthew 13:55-56). Like you, He lived within a family, and the Bible tells us how He grew within that family—in wisdom, in stature, in favor with God and in favor with man (Luke 2:52). This is how you need to grow as well—the same as Jesus.

In Wisdom—Jesus grew in wisdom. Though He was/is deity, Jesus had emptied Himself (Philippians 2:6-8 ASV). I don't know what all that involved, but I do know He gave up heaven and limited Himself, so that He could experience life as a human. Jesus allowed Himself to learn and to grow, just like you must.

In Stature—Jesus was once a baby, then a child, a teenager and finally a man. He felt his body change, had growth spurts like most boys and went through that awkward stage. His voice squeaked and then deepened. Jesus knows what it's like to be young, to have hormones, to feel different and to watch yourself change.

In Favor with God—Jesus is your great example. Even as a teenager, who was He trying to please? His Father. Jesus did not rebel against God. He did not use the excuse that He was young and needed to sow His wild oats. He did not demand things be done His way (Hebrews 5:8; Philippians 2:8). He said, "Thy will be done" (Matthew

26:39). He gained God's favor by always doing what pleased His Father. Would you be like your Savior? Then follow God and His will!

In Favor with Man—Not only did God approve of Jesus but so did man. Those Jesus lived with, those He lived among, looked upon Him with a smile. He was liked. People were glad to see Him come down the street. He was admired in His neighborhood. He didn't mope around like many teens today who claim to be having an identity crisis. Even as a teen, Jesus knew who He was and what His purpose was (Luke 19:10). True, your purpose is not to die and take away the sins of the world. However, your purpose, our purpose is to live for Him, to glorify Him (Psalm 50:23; Matthew 5:16), to live according to His will (Luke 11:28; John 4:34), to do as much good as we can just like our Savior (Galatians 6:9-10; Hebrews 13:16; Romans 12:2), and to prepare ourselves for heaven (2 Peter 3:18; Revelation 20:13, 15). Jesus lived to complete His mission. That did not begin when He was grown; living to please His Father and save our souls began when He was young.

LESSONS FROM JESUS:

In Work—Jesus worked with His father Joseph. He was never spoken of as lazy by his parents or community. Jesus worked to do His heavenly Father's will all His life...until He said, "It is finished" (John 19:30) on the cross.

In Worship—Jesus never missed an opportunity to worship God. He prayed regularly (Luke 18:1). Even at 12 years old He recognized where He should be—in the temple, being about His Father's business (Luke 2:49).

In Life—What did Jesus spend His life doing Good (Acts 10:30). Whether it was His family (John 19:26-27), His friends (John 10:11) or total strangers (Matthew 9:30), the Lord spent His life, filled His life, with good He did for others—so much so that John says the world can't hold the books if Jesus' deeds were all written about (John 21:25)! God help us to be like our Savior and live lives of goodness (Galatians 6:10)!

In Home—Jesus lived in subjection to His parents, just as you should (Colossians 3:20). He was a loving brother to His siblings as well. How do you treat your family? Sometimes we are kinder to strangers than we are to those closest to us. Jesus shows us that even in a humble home of hard work you can be happy, faithful and loving.

DISCUSSION:

1. How much do you worry about what other people think of you? Did Jesus worry about impressing others?

2. What do you want to be when you grow up? Did you think something like "faithful Christian" at all?

3. Jesus had physical temptations just like you do. How did He handle them? What can you do to overcome them?

4. Jesus was never selfish. Most of us are. What do you have to have your way about usually? How can you learn to stop seeking self-satisfaction and start searching for what satisfies others?

5. Look up a verse about humility. How did Jesus' life reflect that? Does yours?

6. What did Jesus teach about forgiveness? (Luke 17:3-4) Give an example of how Jesus practiced what He preached...judging? (Luke 6:41-42, 37) enemies? (Luke 6:27-36)

7. Name three ways you should be more like your Savior.

LESSON 11

Wisdom for Youth from God

God's word has the answers for all life's questions, for all life's problems—for every age. He speaks to each of us. He wants the best for us so He's given us His standard to live by. Our lives will truly be happy *if* we listen!

What does God say to you about:

1. **Youthful lusts**—Psalm 24:3-5 says God will bless the pure. God made our bodies; He gave us desire and drive. But He also tells us how to use these and where to use these properly—in the marriage bond (Hebrews 13:4; Matthew 19:4-9). Did young people in Bible days have the same lusts and problems with sexual sins as we do today? Yes, they did! They must have or why would Paul tell Timothy to flee youthful lusts (2 Timothy 2:22)? Paul knew what the young people were experiencing. It may be difficult but it is what is best for you. And remember— you should care about what pleases God, not yourself.

2. **How you use your tongue**—"Death and life are in the power of the tongue" (Proverbs 18:21). This is certain. Words can kill—relationships, opportunities, even physi- cally. "A fool's mouth is his destruction and his lips are the snare of his soul" (Proverbs 18:7). How do you talk to

your parents? (Proverbs 20:20) Do you curse? Do you lie? Paul says to put off "filthy communication out of you" (Colossians 3:8) and "life not to one another" (verse 9). Not only must you get rid of the negative; you must replace it with the positive, admonishing one another, provoking one another to love and good works and exhorting one another (Colossians 3:16; Hebrews 10:24; Ephesians 4:25).

3. **Laziness**—"Not slothful in business" (Romans 12:11). "Do it heartily as unto the Lord" (Colossians 3:23). God commands in Ecclesiastes 9:10 that whatever our hand finds to do, we do it with all our might. You can't be lazy and please God. Notice this is a command, not a suggestion. Are you lazy at home with chores? In school with homework? If you have a job, do you do just enough to get by? Or do you set an example of hard work to those around you?

4. **Peer pressure**—God says "do not follow a multitude to do evil" (Exodus 23:2). Whose approval do you want? Whose approval is most important? The amazing thing is when you choose not to follow the crowd but rather do what is right, even if it means standing alone, others will often look up to you and admire your individualism. The young people who do this, who do what is right in spite of the crowd, are the truly strong who will be blessed. Don't let the world shape you but "be ye transformed" (Romans 12:2).

5. **Self-discipline**—"A child is known by his doings" (Proverbs 20:11). So are you. Self-discipline is the basis for righteous living. Controlling yourself (that includes controlling your spiritual life) is God's challenge to you. Romans 12:17 says not to recompense evil for evil. We

must control our reactions toward others. Learn to stop and think, then act, not react!

6. **Drinking, drugs, smoking, pornography**—All these stand or fall together, don't they? Does God expect you to have self-control? Does He expect you to be pure and undefiled in body? These verses say He does (Hebrews 12:14; 2 Corinthians 7:1; 2 Peter 1:3-11; James 4:7-8). These are not suggestions!

7. **Dancing**—Lasciviousness is a word we don't use. You'll find it in Galatians 5:19 as one of the works of the flesh. It includes lewd bodily movements. If that doesn't describe the modern dance, what does?! You must not use your body in such a manner. You must use your body to glorify God. But it's fun you say. Yes, but so are lots of sins. Moses called it "the pleasure of sin for a season" (Hebrews 11:25). You must make a choice like he did.

8. **Respect**—Today's society hardly knows this word—respect. What kind of respect do you show to older folks, to your teachers, to all in authority and even to yourself? How do you treat the aged? Your grandparents? Your parents? The elders? Do you know God expects an attitude of respect from you? (Romans 13:7; 12:10; Exodus 20:12; I Peter 2:17; John 5:23; Ephesians 6:1-3)

9. **Humility/Proper Attitude**—God hates "a proud look" (Proverbs 6:17). Are you walking around with your nose in the air, acting as if you are better than everyone else? God hates that. Paul says in Romans 12:3 not to think more highly of yourself than you ought and if you think you are something when you are nothing, you deceive yourself (Galatians 6:3). We must have a balanced view of ourselves. On the one hand, God says we are more valu-

able than all the world and everything in it (Matthew 16:26). After all, Jesus, the very Son of God, shed His blood for YOU! You must be valuable. However, on the other hand, all that you are or ever will be, is because of the grace of God (I Corinthians 15:10). Our value should make us humble, not proud, because we are what we are because of God's love and favor. Pride will bring you down (Proverbs 16:18). It brings destruction and unhappiness. To be truly happy you must esteem others above yourself (Romans 12:10, 16, 18; Philippians 2:4; James 4:10).

LESSONS FROM GOD:

In Home—God expects you to be a good son/daughter, obedient to your parents (Ephesians 6:1).

In Work—If you have a job after school, you should seek to be a hard worker and Christian example to those you work with and for. Remember that you work "as unto the Lord" (Colossians 3:23).

In Life—Don't get discouraged when life gets difficult. Remember that this is your training ground. That's what makes this life, not heaven.

In Worship—Make it your life's commitment to never miss an opportunity to worship God. Can you imagine someone dying to save your life and you not making it to their memorial service? Now consider Jesus. He died to save more than your life. He died to save your very soul. You should feel compelled to thank Him every Lord's Day. Add to that a desire to "seek ye first the kingdom" and you will endeavor to be at every Bible study too! (Hebrews 10:25; Matthew 6:33)

DISCUSSION:

1. Which category do you need to work on the most?

2. Does our culture affect our actions or our beliefs? How?

3. Have you ever destroyed a relationship by saying something you shouldn't have?

4. What does laziness say about other aspects of your character?

5. Give one example of peer pressure you've experienced.

6. Name ways you can show more respect to God and others in your life.

LESSON 12

Review Quiz

Short Answer:

1. What did Daniel do that showed his devotion to God? _____
   _____
   _____
   _____

2. What did Josiah do to the priests of the idols? _____
   _____
   _____
   _____

3. How long was Joseph in prison? _____
   _____

4. Explain how God worked in Joseph's life. _____
   _____
   _____
   _____
   _____

5. What was the result/consequence of David's adultery? _____
   _____
   _____
   _____
   _____

Matching (fill in the blanks with proper number; number may be used more than once):

1. Daniel   2. Joseph   3. Timothy   4. David
5. Josiah   6. Esther   7. Israelite Maid   8. Jesus
9. John Mark   10. Paul's nephew

_____ She saved her people.

_____ He became a ruler in Egypt.

_____ He tore down the idols in Israel when he was only 18.

_____ He grew in stature and in favor with God and man.

_____ He forgave his brothers.

_____ She shared a prophet's gift with her captor.

_____ He became Paul's helper after causing an argument.

_____ He cut off a Philistine's head.

_____ He saved Paul's life.

_____ He was a king, a shepherd, and a murderer.

_____ He was converted by Paul on his first missionary journey.

_____ He was captured by the Babylonians.

_____ Paul called him his beloved son.

_____ His best friend was Jonathan.

_____ He repaired the house of the Lord.

What Do You Think?

1. What lesson was most important to you in this study? Why? ____
    _____
    _____
    _____
    _____
    _____

2. Which Bible character in this study did you like best and why? __
    _____
    _____
    _____
    _____
    _____

3. Choose a Bible verse or passage used in this study and explain its significance to you. _____
    _____
    _____
    _____
    _____

4. How has this study helped you in your Christian life? _____
    _____
    _____
    _____
    _____
    _____

Made in the USA
Middletown, DE
10 September 2024

60041844R00033